Motivating & Empowering Prisoners?

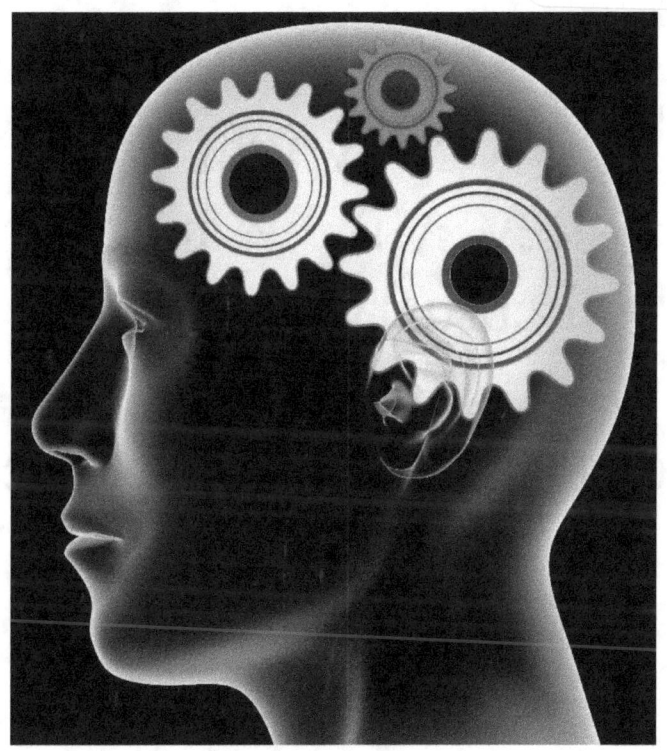

Invite Prisoners To Find Their Motivation & Their Future

Rev. Mike Wanner

Table Of Contents

Introduction

Some sources report that in America alone there are more than 2.3 million people in jail. What motivates that many people?

The Answer is not simple or directly clear. That uncertainty is not helpful to folks who would like to help the prisoners or the situation.

I, like most people, was oblivious to that fact. I started channeling Angel Raphael in 2013 and releasing little message sets at they came through.

In message set 16 of the Angel Raphael Speaks Series there was a message that invited my attention

Here is that message –

"I asked Mike to Step into Prison Energetically

I have asked Mike to get the address and location within a prison of a designated space so he can visit energetically and receive feedback for us. Whether he will have time, interest or opportunity to do this will be interesting to see. As he writes this, he is not thrilled with the idea. We are already consuming a lot of his time."   ARS16

I embraced the invitation in 2016. So far, The Angel Raphael prodding has had me publish the following books related to prisons:

1. Angel Raphael Speaks Volume 4: Angels, Addicts, Alcoholics & Prisoners - Oh Yeah!
2. Angel Raphael Speaks Volume 5: Prisoners Caring for Alcoholics - Australia In Miniature Projects Intro
3. Angel Raphael Speaks Volume 6: Prisoners Caring for Addicts - Australia In Miniature For Addicts
4. Prison Jobs Now: Providing Care For Addicts And Alcoholics
5. Angel Raphael Speaks - Prisons (A Kindle only book -2013)
6. Contained Care Communities: Concept
7. Australia In Miniature
8. Prison Possibilities Dialogue Series: Concept
9. Prison Possibilities Dialogue Series: Volume 2 Dialogues
10. Prison Possibilities Dialogue Series: Volume 3 Dialogues
11. Prison Possibilities Dialogue Series: Volume 4 Dialogues
12. Prison Possibilities Dialogue Series: Volume 5 Dialogues
13. Prison Possibilities Voluntary Exile: Concept
14. Prison Possibilities Correction Coaches: Concept
15. Prison Possibilities for Mexicans: Is A Boat Better than A Wall?
16. Prison Possibilities Family Time: A Reason to Thrive!
17. Prison Genius Pool: "So Much Genius In Jail"
18. Prison Possibilities Access Systems: Prisoner Access by Request
19. Prisoner's Lawyers Can Save The American Economy: Make A Buck Doing It & Be Thanked!
20. Prisoner Family Talks, Days, Stays & Vacations: Connecting Helps Healing
21. Prisoner Writing Projects: Write To Heal, Start Over & Reconnect
22. Prison Cell Clearing & Blessing: Clear Entities, Chase Ghosts, and & Create Sacred Space
23. Prisoner Professors: Show You Are Aware Create Change With Care
24. Prison Reiki? Maybe Someday? A Gateway To Help Heal Prisons & America?
25. Judges and An Angel Rule On Possibilities: We Can Cut Sentences & Prison Costs

This book continues to carry the potential for rethinking that can help to reduce incarceration to those who society needs to have there. I have a concern that many who are in prison are there because of bureaucratic inconsistencies that entangle them in a dysfunction that benefits no one and hurts many prisoners, prison staff, prisoner's families, prison staff's families and many others which specifically includes the taxpayers.

I want to trigger mindset shifts in the prisoners as well as prison employees and the whole community. We need a lot more Objective Productive Dialogues about Enhancing the lives of Prison Employees, Prisoners, Taxpayers and the Families of Each of these groups.

As I have been writing my books on Prisons, the complexity of the process has amazed me. I have some ideas of ways that might help, but I surrender to guidance.

My guidance suggests that we need everybody's ideas. Great strides will be made when creativity is embraced with open minds on both sides of every issue.

1 - Why I am Writing This Book

Open mindedness is a real key point for progressing from the limitations of prison now as closed minds may be one of the leading causes of the resistance that exists. Consider any argument that you ever had and remember that accommodation usually follows a gesture of respect.

My perspective has been hard to achieve but there seems to be hope in understanding, and this book invites ideas to motivate the sharing of ideas that can be good for all.

Like our country, the prison communities seem to need an infusion of objectivity and hope for a better tomorrow. If I were not hopeful, I would not be writing all these books.

I am also practical, and I know that this will take a lot of time but that could be accelerated if there were some graciousness and reasonableness on all sides of everything. I do realize that statement may be challenging to some readers and may have some people disconnect from my message but I want results over the long term, and the simplest and most gracious way of doing that is a team effort where everybody benefits.

We need to deal with hard realities in a way that can soften the problems for us all. There are a lot of hard reasons why understanding does not flow like a river, but I for one am not thrilled with what I read and hear and feel about the situation.

Many of my books above call for prisoners to step up and speak out but that can have consequences both good and bad so the tradition is not likely to change quickly or easily so I would like to propose an effort for understanding and role playing in a program I will call – Let's Change Prison.

Let's do some role playing so that understanding can flow. While I would not call the effort a debate team, I would suggest that the prisons have discussion teams where the goal is not to score points but to strive for comprehension of those whose viewpoint is different.

2 - Prison Change Team Selection

We will want to select wisely those who have the temperament to be diligent and methodical investigators of possibilities for change who can hold their temper and polish words to the degree that common sense can flow freely.

Let's call our team members Discussion Diplomats who will endeavor to dig deep into unseen entanglements and propose new paths of possibilities that they would like to present for the community to embrace.

We will not be able to hold these diplomats accountable for any lack of success because the likelihood of success is remote unless they are each creative and collectively able to integrate that creativity in an area of potential which could produce new results.

Now the complicating factor for such an effort will be the inherent lack of openness within the prison community and the positional opposition between the prisoners and the facility staff.

So to recap, any team members that step up to seek confirmation will have their hands full and should think long and hard before they step up.

3 - Prisoner Motivation Is Hard To Measure

Most of the people on the outside do not understand what is going on behind the walls because things are just so complicated with such huge numbers of jurisdictions. It seems there are more than TWO Million Prisoners in more than **6,000 Correctional Centers** just in the United States.

Prisoners and their families probably do not care about the complexity of understanding for those on the outside, but you might wish to rethink that position. While prisoners and their families may seem to have limited options, there are efforts to Change Prisons and balance resources versus other demands on the government bodies.

High Prison costs may block a lot of things needed in a community and may negatively impact many quality of life as well as life sustaining programs. Lowering Incarceration can help community budgets as well as help the prisoners released and their families.

Discussion Diplomats can support the existing efforts, incentivize precise future effort with critical information and simplify readiness for progress on all fronts.

4 - Building Blocks to Understanding

Anybody willing to take on this agenda will need to have their emotional fortitude (called guts). I will propose a starting point concept from which you or they can build.

Concept

Let me share up front that I am not encouraging new façades that appear to represent prisoners as if they have refreshed spiritually. Instead, I am proposing the Discussion Diplomats dig in and invite prisoners to go deeper into their struggles, determine what experiences in life took them down a road that they would not choose again and share their experiences to warn others not to do what they did.

Sharing Pain

Digging deep and sharing could help a lot of other people to avoid prison. What a gift that would be to both troubled youth and the whole rest of the Country.

The experiences of many prisoners that took them down the wrong path may not be rooted in malice or evil. It may be rooted in emotional misunderstanding and fragmented families.

Regardless of the causes or triggers within a person, a guilty decision by a court is probably not wanted by anybody. Worse still, there could be self-judgment that could be crippling to some prisoners who stop moving forward.

I invite all who have that self-judgment issue to dig into this opportunity and learn from each other's life so the common struggle gives value to each participant so that there may be enough reason to allow them to forgive themselves. When you can find that forgiveness, you may be surprised by the freedom that comes with it.

It may be that you only crave wide open spaces and freedom. The most important thing needed to get it may be understanding, acceptance, personal forgiveness and the willingness to do what you can to make your life count and freedom reign.

You can start to help others and the system and the community by starting with yourself and building progressively.

I suggest that you consider doing all the following:
Find Your Secret That Makes No Sense
Ask if a Trigger Happened? If Yes, When?
Write Your Story As You See It
What To Include In Your Story:
Where You Are
Obstacles To Change You See
Eliminate Your Limitations
Write A New Story
Your Purpose
Attitude Is Everything When Working with People
Write what you would Teach the Inner City Kids
about how to survive and thrive in the City
Be a Professor from Hard Knocks University
Who Can You and How You Can Help?
Share that you care and invite others to learn.

5 - The Secret That Makes No Sense

As you go about the investigation of that which is, you can experience many things that seem to make no sense. The illusion of no-sense can be as simple as a perception within a limited expectation of what is.

We can sometimes see things that are not there and not see things that are because we have expectations that may seem helpful at some times to shortcut the process. The reality of what we think we see has more power over us than the reality that we did not see correctly.

This illusion applies to everyday experiences and especially to highly stimulated multi-action situations. You have probably heard many witnesses describe an auto accident and be surprised that their descriptions may sound like different events.

The human mind is influenced by physical, emotional, mental and spiritual stimuli. While we may think that we are clear about everything that we take as truth, we may be in error.

I once worked with a client, and we determined that an issue for her was a traumatic episode which happened in the womb. The situation was so extreme because her mother was in a crisis.

The damage was also impactful as it created a dissociative state for the unborn baby which made her prone to dissociate again and create a multiple-personality situation. By the time I worked with her, there had been two more splits, so it wound up where she had the three alter egos that complicated her ability to understand and cope with her emotional crises.

13

She also had to deal with her conscious self in the now. I feel that some prisoners have a dissociative experience like PTSD that can have a dissociative effect similar to the client above.

Disassociation is more common than we might think as most people do it to a lesser degree on a more frequent basis. Nietzsche has been quoted saying "Was mich nicht umbringt, macht mich starker. (That which does not kill me, makes me stronger.)"

Just because I stated an example of what might have been like an experience that you might have had, her struggle and yours do not change the law and any accountability that you have or had. The reason that I shared this whole chapter is to explain that the whole world is moving independently. Many things going on that are separate from the experience of each of us.

Please know that another component that I wish you to process is that unfairness does not change a fact. The most important idea is that your possibilities only stop when you quit or give up trying or react in aggressive ways that complicate your circumstances further.

I encourage you to milk the cow of life for every bit of joy that is attainable while you are here as you hopefully are considerate and respectful of everybody else's rights and positions so that new optimism and support can be in your future. No guarantees but what goes around can well return to sender. Consider sending good and kindness, and hopefully, that will return.

6 - Your Story

When you speak, you are also listening to what you say, and then you may believe what you said. So if you say the wrong thing about yourself, you create a story and part of your life that is unreal.

You can change your story at any time, so I encourage you to start the process of understanding by answering a few things about your life.

When do you feel peaceful?_____
Is there a certain something that triggers you to lose peacefulness?_____
Are you doing a certain things immediately prior to a good or bad experience?_____
Do you journal your experiences?_____
Are you willing to journal your experiences?_____
Are you willing to sit and write your whole Story?_____
Do you believe that God can help you if you will open to connect? _____
Will you schedule time in each week to start your story journal now? _____

Why Your Story Is Important

A house is constructed on a foundation and if the foundation is a mess then so will be the rest of the house. Your life is built on your foundation, so you need to be sure it receives the support it needs from time to time.

It is tough to objectively view your foundational story when you are actively inside it. There is great value in stopping the clock metaphorically and recording where you are to the best of your ability in a particular moment.

Your story now does not limit you in any way. It is like intersection signs that show you where you are. Staying at your story intersection can limit you, so I do not recommend it.

If you get stuck in now and have no target destination, you can't go where you have not decided to go. Unfortunately, many people arrive at a story intersection and get stuck there for a considerable time. I do not recommend it.

Getting stuck is not limited to any particular group of people. Movie Stars are as vulnerable as you, military people, business executives, doctors, teachers, and housekeepers.

Imagine that all kinds of people in your community have experiences from different sources and you may never know their story. Know that each of them may be able to say something that can help you. Listen. You may learn a lot free.

Know also that you can reciprocate by paying attention to their needs so that you can at least offer them your understanding which may be life-saving to them or you. It may be difficult for you to imagine but one word of encouragement at a pivotal time can save a life.

Saving another can help you see your value to the world. When you are giving to others, you gain your respect and then you do not need for others to respect you but they will.

Buddy Up

If you read a buddy's foundational story journal, you could quickly see that there is a clear path in which to move. Since you are not involved, it is easier for you to understand issues easier and be more objective than the writer.

If that same buddy reads your journal, s/he can objectively see the next little step that you need to take. Both you and your friend have new information as you move down your paths in route to your optimized destination.

Why the Questions?

So let's consider the why of the questions asked above:

1. When Do You Feel Peaceful?

It is important to understand the timing of your experiences as it is a component that can frame some patterns that you might misunderstand without that reference.

2. Is there a certain something that triggers your experiences?

If an experience is always preceded by a predictable triggering, control of the trigger events can be a tool to change the experience. Acknowledgment of your triggers can be comforting to you as you know what to avoid so that you are triggered less often.

3. Are you doing a certain thing immediately before an experience?

What you are doing before an episode that is not perceived as a trigger may also be a path to a trigger situation which while it is not an immediate cause can be a preparatory step that sets the stage for an experience which can then be activated by any number of otherwise inconsequential things.

4. Do You Journal Your Experiences?

Journaling your experiences is a great tool to help yourself or any practitioner that you are working with at the time. Professional time is very expensive, but your notes can cut short the process of information gathering that they need to attain a baseline for where you are at the starting point.

5. Are you willing to journal your experiences?

Knowing you could and doing journaling are two entirely different things. If you are serious about healing, begin to do the journaling as it is a taking charge type of decisive effort that says to yourself that you are serious about healing and you will take the initiative to do whatever it takes to heal.

6. Are you willing to sit and write your whole Story?

Being ready to write your story is the beginning point of a Journey of self- discovery. Now, is not a time to be careful about hiding the truth from your self.

If you are concerned about somebody finding and reading your story, then take precautions to protect it wherever it physically is, or password protects it if it is on your computer or a community computer. A good way to satisfy yourself that it is safe is to put somebody else's name on it. Billy Smith's Journal or Gladys Jones 's journal is not yours, and you can deny it if it is found. Don't use the name of someone you know as that could get awkward or problematic.

7. Do You Believe That God Can Help You If You Open To Connect?

God can help you if you invite God. Some folks have reservations about God and can block the good that God offers.

You beliefs are a big part of your healing, and too much doubt can knock your success out. Don't play games. You are too important.

7 - What To Include In Your Story

Share a detailed account of where you came from and what the situation is now. Include cultural references to your family ancestry, education, family business, religion, chronic family illnesses, marital status, etc.

As you review the list of items below, try to be aware of the emotions that come up and record them. Especially include feelings of heartache, betrayal, anger, fear, and rage. Consider if the following influence your old story:

Race
Age
Living Locations
Education
Family culture
Family Business
Religious Upbringing
Family Illnesses
Marital Status
Military Service
Identified Traumas/Crimes
Medical History with Ages
Drug Dependency – Prescription
Drug Dependency – Street Drugs
Smoking
Alcohol Use
Family Crisis – Immediate Family
Family Crisis – Extended Family
Sexual History and Experiences

8 - Where You Are

You have been dealt a hand in life. If you are not Royalty, You may not like it.

If you don't like it, Get real and Change the Deal. Drop the "'T" off "I can't" and make it "I can"

It's your life, you are in charge, and you are the dealer. Shuffle the cards and begin to play within your own rules.

But you may say – "How Can I change things?" That's simple: You change them by thinking about them differently.

Start walking on the path to Release. Acknowledge how you feel. Undo the lock that stress has on you by owning your feelings and asking for help. Who do you ask?

You may wish to say "God Help Me change."

You may not. Some people understand about God, whoever and whatever you believe God to be, and others just don't.

You can change things a lot easier with God's help, but that is not for everyone, so I cover many ideas. You always have a choice in life even when it feels that you do not.

9 - Elimination of Limitations

Here is the technique for the Elimination of Limitations.

MAKE A LIST OF YOUR "I CANT'S" Spend some time on it. Make certain you have them all.

Grade each with a priority code. Grade each A, B, C, D. A will equal the worst of the worst or you could say your best of the "I cant's, " or you could say the things you absolutely can't do. Put them down on the list.
B will equal the next level of difficulty.
C will equal the next level of difficulty.
D will equal the least difficult things that you can't do.

Next, prioritize them in descending order from 10 (the worst) to 1 (the least) within their alphabetical grade. You would have A10 to A1, B10 to B1, C10 to C1, D10 to -D1. Yes, you can have more that one of each but if you have a lot of one then you will need to further prioritize with sub-lists.

Print or write out the list in descending priority order.

You have done all that work pat yourself on the back. You are working at taking charge of your life. There are few more noble tasks. You are polishing the diamond that you are.

You are creating sparkle in your life, your family and your community. You are on your way to your power. Now get to work on this list.

Start with the Least D1. Get a pen or pencil (red if you have it) and take your D1 and make an x over the "'T" or get an eraser (Liquid or rubber) and remove the "'T." Make the remaining "I can" your affirmation for three days at least or as many as 21. "I can _____. " Say it at least three times a day, preferably a lot more. Take some action (one step minimum each day) towards the fulfillment of D1. Notice how it feels to do that.

Next, start with the worst. Get a pen or pencil (red if you have it) and take your A10 and make a red x over the "'T." or get an eraser (liquid or rubber) and remove the "'T." Make the remaining "I can" your affirmation for three days at least or as many as 21. "I can _____. " Say it at least three times a day, preferably a lot more. Take some action (one step minimum each day) towards the fulfillment of A10. Notice how it feels to do that.

Take your next lowest and then your next highest. Etc.

WOW! After all that work, it is time to reward yourself. Remember to be gentle with yourself as you work to polish the diamond that you are.

10 - Write A New Story

When you have finished working on polishing the diamond that you are, You can create for yourself a story of how you would like your life to be. Take every bit of new freedom from the work you just finished above and write the new story with your clearing and eliminations fully implemented.

Tell the tale of your power and manifestations as completely as you can envision. Put down every detail as vibrantly as you can.

You have done a lot if you are following my instructions. You have found out where you are and formed new thought patterns as to what you can do.

You have started the process of changing your thinking to align with a new reality that will be much more to your liking. You have created a vision of the path that will take you to your new success destination.

Congratulations. You have done a lot, and your new story can serve you well and open many doors for you.

For
Considering
These
Ideas

Ever

It Does Not Help Prayer Still Does!

13 - Resource Books

Distant Healing Sessions (or Join Mail List) – Write To mikewann@voicenet.com

Books by Rev. Mike at www.Amazon.com

Veterans Healing Six Pack
1. *Trauma Healing Options for VA Hospitals: Help for Veterans to Own Their Healing and their future.*
2. *Trauma Healing Action Steps for Veterans: Help to Start Healing*
3. *Trauma Healing Action Steps for Veterans: Empowerment*
4. *Trauma Healing Action Steps for Veterans: Forgiveness*
5. *Trauma Healing Action Steps for Veterans: Thought Freedom*
6. *Tea For Veterans: Welcome One Home*

PTSD Power Pack:
1. *The PTSD Project: Turn Pain To Power*
2. *PTSD & Soul Retrieval: Putting One Back Together*
3. *PTSD & The Purple PAD: Calling all Scientists and PTSD Patients*

Angel Raphael Speaks Volume 1: Take Courage! God Has Healing in Store for You!
Angel Raphael Speaks Volume 2: Take Courage! God Has Healing in Store for You!
Angel Raphael Speaks Volume 3: Take Courage! God Has Healing in Store for You!
Angel Raphael Speaks Volume 4: Angels, Addicts, Alcoholics & Prisoners – Oh Yeah!
Angel Raphael Speaks Volume 5: Prisoners Caring for Alcoholics - Australia In Miniature Projects Intro
Angel Raphael Speaks Volume 6: Prisoners Caring for Addicts - Australia In Miniature For Addicts
Reiki Journaling from Japan
Reiki Is Alive: God's Great Gift
Four Parts to Healing
Distant Healing: We Are All Connected
Stress Release Energy Work: How To Cope
Does Reiki Love Heal Cancer?
Group Consciousness
Salute To Philadelphia VA Medical Center: Thank You
Reiki Transcript for Reiki 2 & 3 Channels: Dr. Usui Is That You?
God Bless Kindle & Amazon
Puppies Are Different From People
If Your Dog Dies
Toy Guns Are Obsolete

Great Spirit Made Children With Red Skin: AND
The Cage of Fear: Is Not Locked
God Made Children Red, Yellow, Brown, Black & White: Greet Each Child With
Kindness
Emergency Medical Kindness In The Cradle Of Liberty: Big City - Cracked Bell
Angels Are Always Around Addicts and Addicts: Help Is Near Now! Invite It In!
Angels Are Always Around Addicts and Alcoholics: Volume 2 - Tools To Help Re-Light
Your Life
Prison Jobs Now: Providing Care For Addicts And Addicts
Controlled Care Communities Concept
Prison Possibilities Dialogue Series: Concept
Prison Possibilities Dialogue Series: Volume 2, 3, 4, 5 Dialogues
Prison Possibilities Voluntary Exile
Prison Possibilities Corrections Coaches
Prison Possibilities For Mexicans: Is A Boat Better Than A Wall?
Prison Possibilities Family Time: A Reason to Thrive!
Prison Genius Pool: "So Much Genius In Jail"
Prison Possibilities Access Control: Prisoner Access by Request
Prisoner's Lawyers Can Save The American Economy: Make A Buck Doing It & Be
    Thanked!
Prisoner Family Talks, Days, Stays & Vacations: Connecting Helps Healing
Prisoner Writing Projects: Write To Heal, Start Over & Reconnect
Prison Cell Clearing & Blessing: Clear Entities, Chase Ghosts, and & Create Sacred
Space
Prisoner Professors: Show You Are Aware Create Change With Care
Prison Reiki? Maybe Someday? A Gateway To Help Heal Prisons & America?
Judges and An Angel Rule On Possibilities: We Can Cut Sentences & Prison Costs
Ideas For Prison Wardens: Leadership Is Not Easy
Solitary Community: Could Community Support Cut Costs and Issues?

Little Books at Kindle.com by Rev. Mike:
English Medical History Questionnaire For Non-English Speakers
English Language Helper For Non-English Speakers
Wise Wonderful Women Are The Well Of The Family
Answers for Test & Research: Dowsing Power
Crisis? Reiki! Baby? Reiki!
Bible References For Healing
Angel Raphael Speaks – Prisons
Angel Raphael Speaks – Veterans
The Saint Off Interstate 95

14 - Angels Please Prayers

Addict's

Angels of Healing Selected
Help Me to Stay Directed
Come To Me From The Sky
I Am Ready to Succeed Not Try
If I Don't Invite You In
I Might Not Win
I Have Been Lost For Too Long
Help Me To Stay Strong

Alcoholic's

Angels of Healing On High
Help Me to Stay Dry
Come To Me From The Sky
I Am Ready to Succeed Not Try
If I Don't Invite You In
I Might Not Win
I Have Been Lost For Too Long
Help Me To Stay Strong

From

15 - Private Channeling

Angel Raphael Speaks a series of free messages that are channeled through Reverend Mike Wanner for the Highest good and Highest Healing of all concerned.

Many questions arise about Reverend Mike doing private channeling, and he does help with that so e-mail him.

Reverend Mike is available worldwide as a psychic channel, emotional release facilitator, spiritual energy practitioner & teacher, and public speaker. He looks forward to meeting you soon!

Email - mikewann@voicenet.com 215-342-1270 PRIVATE SPIRITUAL READINGS/channelings or Spiritual Healing Sessions: Telephone or in person. Rev. Mike is available for private, one-on-one intuitive sessions with you, his Guide Family, and your Guides. He helps by offering clarity on emotional situations about your life, your purpose, your spirituality, and the release of stuffed emotions and cellular memory.
Connect to the love of your Guides today!
Contact Rev. Mike for an appointment.
Sessions available:

Spiritual Readings
Angel Channeling
Distant Reiki Healing
Distant Clearing of Stuffed Emotions
Distant Clearing Cellular Memory
Distant Clearing Energy Blockages
Distant Clearing of the Chakras
Customized needs
Mastermind dowsing responses to yes/no direction finding questions.

Rev. Mike is a facilitator of healing. He brings you and the Divine together so that you can align with the Divine and have a great time and a great life. All healing is between you and God, as it should be. Go ahead and start without Rev. Mike. Visit his prayer site http://www.Create-A-Prayer.com. Take the first step NOW.

16 - Reverend Mike Wanner

Rev. Mike Wanner started his metaphysical and ministerial studies with Reiki in 1993 and had studied seven styles of Reiki in the U.S., Japan, Canada, Denmark and Australia. He is certified to teach. He became certified to teach Integrated Energy Therapy in 1999 and co-taught the first IET class of the new Millennium. Mike began dowsing in 2001.

Ordained as a Metaphysical Minister of the International Metaphysical Ministry and an Interfaith Minister of the Circle of Miracles Ministry, Rev. Mike practices and teaches spiritual energy therapies in the Philadelphia Area.

Rev. Mike holds ministerial degrees from the University of Metaphysics and the University of Sedona. He is a Pastoral Care Associate of Aria - Frankford Hospital. He taught at the National Academy of Massage Therapy and Health Sciences.

Rev. Mike was a faculty member of the Medical Mission Sister's Center for Human Integration's School of Integrated Body/Mind Therapies in Fox Chase, Philadelphia, PA for twelve years.

Rev. Mike is licensed by the teaching of Intuitional Metaphysics to practice Spiritual Healing and Scientific Prayer. Mike is also a Prayer therapist.

Rev. Mike was elected in 2007 to the status of "Fellow of the American Institute of Stress."

In 2008, Rev. Mike became a practitioner of Coincidental Recognition as he incorporated the CoRe System into his spiritual healing practice.

In 2009, Rev. Mike trademarked a new healing process called Quantum Quatro! Subtle Energy System Support®.

In 2011, Rev. Mike joined the outreach program known as the Health Advantage Group.

In 2012, Rev. Mike became a Certified Professional Coach by The Master Coaching Academy and Joined the Personal Empowerment Group.

Before his metaphysical, ministerial and coaching studies, Rev. Mike worked for Sears Roebuck and Co. while in High School and after graduation, until he joined the U. S. Air Force in 1965. He returned to Sears from Vietnam in 1969 and stayed until 1978. His final Sears assignment was as an efficiency expert in Methods - Operational Research and Development.

He volunteered with Burholme Emergency Medical Services from 1969 and is still a Life Member and Board of Directors Member. He started a private ambulance company in 1975 and worked professionally in the field until 2001 when he devoted his full attention to real estate investing, healing, coaching, and writing.